Rookie
reader®

Dance, Annie

Children's Press®
A Division of Grolier Publishing
New York • London • Hong Kong • Sydney
Danbury, Connecticut

For Eva, who dances with me in the living room
—D. F.

To my mother
—N. i. d. B.

Reading Consultant
Katharine A. Kane
Education Consultant
(Retired, San Diego County Office of Education
and San Diego State University)

Visit Children's Press® on the Internet at:
http://publishing.grolier.com

Library of Congress Cataloging-in-Publication Data

Friedman, Dawn.
   Dance, Annie / by Dawn Friedman ; illustrated by Nicole in den Bosch.
      p. cm. — (Rookie reader)
   Summary: Annie performs a variety of dances in her recital as she blows
in the wind, twirls, taps her toes, and strikes a pose.
   ISBN 0-516-22233-3 (lib. bdg.)   0-516-27289-6 (pbk.)
   [1. Dance—Fiction. 2. Stories in rhyme.] I. Bosch, Nicole in den, ill. II.
Title. III. Series.
PZ8.3.F9114 Dan 2001
[E]—dc21   00-038428

GROLIER
PUBLISHING   1 2 3 4 5 6 7 8 9 10 R 10 09 08 07 06 05 04 03 02 01

Annie loves
to dance!

Stretch your legs.
Hold the wall.

Twirl, standing tall.

Twirl, standing tall.

Blow in the wind.

Swing your partner.

Tap your toes.

13

Hear the beat.

Strike a pose.

Every dance was
so much fun.

Annie danced . . .

in every one!

Word List (32 words)

a	legs	tall
Annie	loves	tap
beat	much	the
blow	one	to
dance	partner	toes
danced	pose	twirl
every	so	wall
fun	standing	was
hear	stretch	wind
hold	strike	your
in	swing	

★ ★ ★ ★ ★ ★ ★ ★ ★ ★ ★

About the Author

Dawn Friedman is a former dancer and dance teacher who lives in suburban Chicago with her husband and daughter. She has choreographed LOTS of dance recitals!

About the Illustrator

Nicole in den Bosch has been busy the past seven years designing children's displays around the country and the world. She lives in Annapolis, Maryland, with her dog, Pooh Bear, where she devotes her time to illustration and playing outside. Apart from illustrating children's books, she also works for the stationery and giftware industry, doing all sorts of illustration projects from greeting cards to paper products.